Bacchylides

Bacchylides

Contents

I	7
II	13
III	17
IV	22
V	24
VI	27
VII	30
VIII	31
IX	34
IX	36

BACCHYLIDES

BY
Bacchylides

I

The following ode celebrates a victory in the horſe races at Olympia won by Hiero, tyrant of Syracuſe, at ſome period between 5oo and 450 B.C. The ſame viſtory is the ſubject of one of Pindar's extant odes. What Hiero had to do with Hercules or Meleager is a aueſtion which muſt be left to the conjecture of the reader, as to which the translator can offer little or no affiance. There were doubtleſs tragic incidents in the career of Hiero; and Bacchylides, after remarking that no human proſperity is unalloyed, proceeds to relate that even the invincible ſon of Zeus had certain adventures far from joyous.

HIGH-DESTINED lord of car-borne Syra-cuſans, thou canſt rightly judge, if any living mortal can, the violet-crowned Muſes' dulcet ſtrains: and now, reſting awhile from cares of ſtate, turn hither thy attention, and pronounce whether the low-cindtured Graces helped to weave his lay the gueft who comes to your famed city from Zea's facred ifle. A votary of golden-filleted Urania he fain with his own voice would fing the praifes of Hiero. High aloft cleaving the deeps of ether with fleet tawny wings, the eagle, meffenger of Zeus, wide-ruling thunderer, boldly travels, confident in matchlefs might, where lefler warblers fear to venture. Neither peaks of the vafty earth nor dangerous billows of the ever-reftlefs main ftay him, but onward through the abyfs of heaven with fine-fpun plumage he fweeps, his fole companion Zephyr, con-fpicuous to mortal gaze. I too have myriad paths, by the grace of dark-haired Victory and of brazen-mailed Ares, to celebrate your praifes, Oh illuftrious fons of Dinomenesj on whom may heaven never ceafe to fmile.

Cheftnut-hued Pherenicus, ftorm-footed fteed, was witnefled victorious by golden-fingered dawn both by the fair ftream of Alpheus and on the haunted meads of Pytho: and by holy Earth I fwear, never duft from rival hoof has foiled him when he neared the goal. Fleet as the north wind's blaſt, and docile to the rein, along ſhouting nations he ſpeeds winning victory or hoſpitable Hiero. Call a mortal happy to whom heaven metes a ſhare of triumph, an envied ſtation, and a life of pomp: abſolutely bleſſed there is none of earth's children.

Even he who levelled many a hoſtile tower, the unconquerable ſon of Zeus who hurls the flaming thunderbolt, deſcended, they ſay, to the infernal halls of fair Perſephone, to drag from Hades to the light of day the iron-jawed monſter, whelp of deadly-fanged Echidna. There he ſaw the ſouls of hapleſs mortals by the waters of Cocytus, like leaves that the north-weſt wind drives up and down the ſheepbrowzed ſpurs of Ida. Among them gleamed conspicuous, wielding a ſpear, the lifelike form of a dauntleſs warrior, grandchild of Porthaon. Him in refulgent armour noting, Alcmeria's heroic ſon brought the ſhrill-twanging cord to his bow's curved tip, oped his quiver and took thereout a brazen-headed ſhaft; when forward ſtepped the ſhade of Meleager, and thus addreſſed him, knowing whom he ſaw: 'Son of mighty Zeus, ſtay where thou art, and with ſerener mind forbear to vainly launch a hoftile bolt at fouls of the dead. No foe confronts thee.' So fpake he. Aftonifhed ftood Amphi-tryo's princely fon, and cried : ' What mortal or immortal fire—what region—reared fuch a fcion? and what hand flew him? Perad-venture fair-cinctured Hera will fend the fame adverfary againft my life. But that is a concern for Pallas of the yellow hair.' Him answered Meleager, his cheek bedewed with tears: 'Hard it is for mortals to bend the refolution of the gods. Elfe had car-borne Oeneus allayed the ire of high, flower-crowned, white-armed Artemis, fupplicating, fond fire, with facrifices of many goats and many tawny-hided oxen. But unappeafable was the wrath of the goddefs. She fent, huntrefs maiden, a monfter boir of undaunted fiercenefs into the lovely dales of Calydon; where, refiftlefs in its might, it felled orchards with its tufks, flaughtered fleecy flocks, and every mortal it encountered. With it we, picked band of Hellas, waged defperate battle for fix days without ftay; and when high heaven gave Aetolia victory, we fet ourfelves to bury thofe whom the tufked monfter had flain in furious onfet, Ancaeus and Agelaus, beft of my dear brothers born of

Althaea in the far-famed halls of Oeneus. But ftill more warriors were doomed to fall, for the offended huntrefs daughter of Latona had not yet ceafed her wrath, and we joined fierce battle with the valiant Curetes for the boar's tawny hide. There among many others I flew Iphiclus and good Aphareus my mother's gallant brethren. For fierce Ares makes no diftincion of friend or foe, but fliafts fly blindly at oppofing ranks, carrying death wher-ever fortune wills. The sore-ftricken daughter of Theftius remembered not this, and—ah haplefs mother—refolved my death—ah paffion-governed woman. She dragged from rich-carved cafket and kindled the quickly burning brand that at my birth fate doomed to be coeval with my days. At the moment I was ftripping of his arms Clymenus, valiant fon of Deipylus, a youth of noble build, whom I had overtaken outfide the walls, when the Curetes fled to the goodly towers of ancient Pleuron. A fudden faintnefs feized my foul; I felt my ftrength decline, alas; and with lateft breath wept to feel life's youthful fplendour flitting. Men fay the eye of Amphitryo's fearlefs fon then and never elfe was moiftened by pity for the ill-ftarred hero, as thus he anfwered: ' Mortals' beft fate is never to be born nor ever to behold the fun's bright rays. But nought avails repining: fo let my tongue frame words to mould the future. Remains there in the palace of Oeneus, dear to Ares, any virgin daughter of features like to thine ? Her would I gladly make my honoured bride.' Him anfwered dauntlefs Meleager's fprite:' In her father's houfe I left the fweet-voiced Deianira, unacquainted yet with mortal-charming, golden Aphrodite'

White-armed Calliope, ftay here thy fhapely car. Be now thy theme Zeus, lord of Olym-pus, ruler of gods; the ever-rufhing flood of Alpheus; royal Pelops; and Pifa, whence far-famed Pherenicus returned victor in the race to Syracufa's towers, bringing to Hiero a fure token of heaven's favour. Truth requires us to pufh envy from our bofom with both hands, and praife the mortal who fucceeds. A Boeotian of old days, Hefiod, fervant of the Mufes, faid: ' The man whom the immortals honour fhould be honoured by all mortals.' I readily greet Hiero with aufpicious bodings of profper-ous career, for that has put forth vigorous ftems; which may Zeus, moft mighty fire, ever guard uninjured by the ftorm of war.

II

This ode celebrates the viftory of a native of Metapontum in a wrefling match in the Pythian games at Delphi. The connexion of the victory with the fiory of the Proetides confifis in the fact that the fame Artemis who healed the daughters of Proetus was a deity worf hipped at Metapontum and the victor's patron goddefs. She derived, according to Callimachus, her title 'Healer of the mind' (Hamera) from curing the Proetides of their moonstruck madness.

[A few lines, apoftrophizing Victory, are wanting.]

AND on the golden floor of Olympus, ftationed by the throne of Zeus, thou ad-judgeft rank of merit to mortals and immortals. Hail fair-haired daughter of juft-judging Zeus! By thy grace athletic youths with choral dance and revelry already proclaim Metapontum a heaven-favoured city; hymning the fon of Phaifcus, mark of all eyes, victor in the Pythian games. Him the god whom flowing-robed Latona bore in Delos received with aufpicious glance; and on the head of Alexidamus fell many a wreath of flowers telling of unchequered victory in the rude wreftling match. On that day the fun never faw him fallen on the lap of earth. No, and I will boaft that in facred Pelops' haunted vale by Alpheus ftream, had only Juftice not been made to ftray from her true path, a pale olive wreath won in conteft againft the champions of all Hellas had encircled his brows when he returned to the nurfe of famous fteeds, his native land. [No malice] in that facred vale affailed the youth with tortuous guile, but or fome adverfe god or erring human judgement wrefted the glorious prize from his hands. And now he owes a fplendid triumph to Artemis the golden-fhafted huntrefs, the healer of the mind, the unerring archer; her to whom the fon of Abas and his fair-robed daughters erft built an altar, goal of many worfhippers.

Forth from the fplendid halls of Proetus almighty Hera once drove the maidens under the refiftlefs yoke of madnefs. They with ftill childifh fouls entering the fanctuary of the purple-zoned goddefs, faid that their fire far outflione in wealth her who fits befide the throne of Zeus, majeftic king. She in dif-pleafure darted into their bofoms abhorred illufions, and they fled into the mountain foreft uttering wild bellowing[1], leaving the towers of Tiryns and its god-built ftreets. For 'twas there that, deferting heaven-favoured Argos, dauntlefs brazen-shielded demigods had dwelt full ten years with their all-envied king. For ftrife implacable from flighteft caufe had flaflied into flame between the fons of Abas, the brothers Proetus and Acrifius. Through them the people whom they ruled were afflicted with civil broils, and partifan tribunals, and flaugh-terous ftrife. So they entreated the Abantian brothers to caft lots for the fertile plains, while

[1] Proetides implerunt falfis mugitibus agros.'—VERGIL.

the younger fhould found the city Tiryns, before irreparable ill enfued. And Zeus, imp of Cronos, in regard for the progeny of Danaus and chivalrous Lynceus, vouchfafed to heal the baleful diforder. Audacious Cyclopian builders coming from afar raifed a wondrous wall for a goodly city, and there the godlike heroes dwelt in high renown, having quitted ftoried Argos, birth-place of fleet fteeds. 'Twas thence the dark-treffed virgin daughters of Proetus fled. Anguifh feized the father's heart, crufhed by the ftrange difafter; and he thought to cleave his breaft with two-edged fword; but his fpearman band with foothing words and ftrong hands hindered him. Full thirteen moons the maidens lurked in darkfome forefts and roved over Arcadia's flieep-browzed glens. But when their fire reached Lufus' fair ftream, after laving in its waters he in-voked crimfon-fcarfed Latona's ox-eyed child, with hands uplifted to the fwift-charioteering fun, to heal his children of their dire falfe weening lunacy—cand I will offer thee in facrifice twenty tawny-hided oxen never yet subjected to the yoke.' The daughter of an * almighty fire, the huntrefs maiden, heard his prayer and, perfuading Hera, healed the flower-crowned virgins of their god-forfaken madnefs. They ftraightway enclofed for her a facred grove and reared her an altar, and ftained it with the blood of victims, and inftituted yearly dances of maiden choirs. 'Twas thence that starting, oh golden lady of subject cities, thou wentest with Achaeans dear to Ares to horse-pasturing plains of Italy, and, auspicious fortune in thy train, dwellest in Metapontum; where they gave thee a lovely grove by the banks of deep Casuentus in compensation for thy lost sanctuary, after that by doom of the immortals, leagued with brazen-mailed Atridae, they laid in late ruin Priam's lofty towers. Whoso judges with just mind will find in every age myriad glorious exploits of Achaeans.

III

On the walls of the temple of Theseus at Athens, according to Pausanias, was to be seen a picture representing the last scene of the adventure narrated in the following ode.

In prehistoric days, before Athens was tyrant of the Aegean, she owed to Crete an annual tribute of seven girls and seven boys to be sacrificed to Minotaur, the Cretan monster.

In this ode Bacchylides aſſumes that Minos, the Cretan king, has received the tribute, and Theſeus, the Athenian hero, in ſome unexplained poſition, is on board the veſſel which bears them to Crete. The mention of Athena in the opening lines is of good omen for the captives.

Eriboea in after days was mother of the Aegine-tan hero, Ajax.

Minos' had wedded Paſiphae, daughter of the Sun, as we ſball be reminded in the ode.

A BLUE-PROWED ship, bearing valiant Theſeus and twice ſeven noble children of Ionia, was ſwiftly cleaving Cretan waters. On its far-gleaming ſails fell blaſts of Boreas by the heſt of high, aegis-ſwaying Athena. And magic gifts of the charm-cinċtured goddeſs Aphrodite flung the heart of Minos. He no longer checked a raſh hand, and touched the white cheeks of a maiden. But Eriboea ſhrieked to the brazen-mailed descendant of Pandion. Theſeus beheld, and beneath frowning brows rolled an indignant eye, heart-ftruck with keen pain. And thus he fpoke : ' Son of mighty Zeus, no longer law-revering wifdom rules thy will. Ufe not, oh hero, tyrannous violence. Whatever heaven's refiftlefs doom hath decreed and the fcale of juftice hath impofed, the utmoft of bur pre-defined lot, we will fuffer when it comes. But do thou curb oppreflive purpofe. If a high born maiden, Phoenix' fair child, bride of Zeus beneath the peaks of Ida, made thee by thy birth moft exalted of mortals; me too the daughter of rich Pittheus bore to fea-god Pofeidon, and received as wedding gift a golden veil from violet-garlanded Nereids. Wherefore, king of Cnoflus, I bid thee abftain from deep-wounding outrage. For I would never willingly fee again the charming light of immortal dawn after thou fliouldeft offer diflionour to any of the youths. Ere that happens we will fhow what ftrength is in our arms, and the iffue heaven (hall arbitrate.' Thus fpoke the hero, armed with juftice. Amazed were the crew to hear his overweening rafhnefs-"and he who wived the daughter of the Sun was ftirred to anger. He formed an inftant plan, and cried aloud, 'Mighty ruler, Zeus my fire, lift to my prayer. If in sooth thou beest my sire by Phoenix' white-armed daughter, now send thou down from heaven the swift, fiery-maned lightning, signal all may recognize. And s Troezenian Aethra bore thee also, Theseus, to the earth-shaking god Poseidon, boldly fling thy fair body into thy father's halls, and bring back the golden ring that now decks my finger from the waves' sait abyss. Thou shall see whether my prayer is granted by the imp of Cronos, lord of the lightning, universal king.' Mighty Zeus granted the exorbitant desire, according Minos tran-scendent honour, to give a dear child clear attestation. He hurled the lightning. Minos, valiant hero, when he saw the welcome portent, pointed towards the vault of heaven and said : ' Thou seest, Theseus, the unambiguous response of Zeus, and now do thou leap into the bass-voiced waters, and thy sire, the imp of Cronos, lord Poseidon, {hall give thee glory unparalleled on earth's verdant plains/ So spake he. The other's courage recoiled not, and stepping on to the vessel's shapely stern he leaped, and the deep received him into its liquid forest Then the child of Zeus relented in his inmost soul, and bade them stay the shapely ship that hastened down the wind. But fate purpofed another way. Onward rufhed the rapid barque, fped by a gale of Boreas blowing from the ftern. All the band of young Athenians trembled when the hero leapt into the waves, and gentle eyes dropped tears from hearts that boded dire difafter. But dolphin denizens of the brine fleetly bore ftrong Thefeus to the palace of his fteed-borne fire. He reached the divine abode, and beheld with awe the ftoried daughters of bleffed Nereus; for their beauteous limbs gleamed with fire-like radiance, and their heads were circled with fillets of woven gold, as with lightly-bending feet they difported in joyous dance. He faw in lovely bower his fire's dear confort, majeftic, ox-eyed Amphitrite; who flung upon him a purple mantle, and on his crifp locks fet a wondrous diadem, erft wedding gift from wily Aphrodite, twined with rofes. Nought willed by heaven is incredible to fober-thinking mortals. He arofe at the fhip's narrow ftern before their eyes. Hah! from what tormenting thoughts he delivered the Cnoffian king, when, undrenched by the wave, he climbed the fliip's fide, amazing fpectacle, the divine adorn ments glittering on his limbs. The radiant bench of maidens with new-created courage raifed a loud cry of gladnefs, the fea refounded with the peal, and the boys clofing round them fang a paean with fweet voices. God of Delos, mayeft thou, charmed by the Zean chorus, grant it heavenfent guerdon of applaufe.

IV

The following fong for two voices was probably written for the Athenian Efhebi, the youths who garrifoned the frontier fortrejfes in their fecond year of military fervice.

One of the fpeakers is Aegeus, king of Athens: the other may be Medea, who fled to Athens after taking vengeance on Jafon.

Procoptes is another name for Procruftes, and Polypemon may be his father.

KING of facred Athens, Lord of Ionians who live at eafe, what tidings caufed the brazen-throated trumpet to found a warlike note? Is a hoftile commander croffing the frontier of our land? Or are marauding brigands, defying fliepherds, driving our flocks in lawlefs raid? Or what alarms thy foul? Tell me, for, methinks, if any mortal has valiant warriors to defend him, it is thou, oh offlpring of Pandion and Creufa.

A herald came by land from the far end of the ifthmus bringing tidings of wondrous deeds of fome man of might. He flew proud Sinis, ftrongeft of mortals, begotten by him of Cronos born, the earth-fhaker god, Lytaeus : killed the homicidal boar of the groves of Crommyon, and the ruthlefs bandit Sciron: clofed Cer-cyon's wreftling fchool: and made Procoptes, overmatched, drop Polypemon's heavy hammer. What may be his crowning exploit is my fear.

Who faid he the man was, and whence, and with what train equipped? Said he that he comes with warlike armament and numerous hoft,' or unaccompanied, like merchant wandering in foreign lands, but with ftrength and prowefs and daring fingly to overcome fuch mighty ones? Or has he heaven's miflion to bring vengeance on the wicked? Elfe it were not eafy, ever battling, not to meet with a mifhap. In long fpace of time every ifliie comes to pafs.

He faid that only two men follow him: that from his gleaming fhoulders hangs a fword [. . . .], two polifhed javelins are in his hands: ' a fhapely Spartan helm prefles his auburn locks: a purple tunic and a woollen mantle of Theflaly enfold his breaft: his eyes flafh red volcanic flame: he is in youth's earlieft prime: his delight is in the games of Ares, war and battle's brazen clangour: and his feet are bound for fplendour-loving Athens.

V

This ode celebrates a victory at Nemea by a native of Phlius. The river Afopus on which Phlius flood was the mythical father of many daughters who gave their names to various cities and iflands, e.g. Thebes, Aegina, Salamis, &c. After touching on the origin of the Nemean games and the victor's deeds, Bacchy-lides-feems about to launch on fome Theban mythology when the fragment ends abrupt-

ly.

When Adraſtus, king of Argos, and the other 'Seven againſt Thebes' were at Nemea on their march to aſſiſt the exiled Polynices to recover his throne, the death of the child Archemorus was recognized by the ſon of Oecleus, the prophet Am-phiaraus, one of the Seven, as an omen of diſaſter, and he vainly urged his companions to abandon the enterprise.

Achilles traced his lineage, through Peleus, Aea-cus, and Aegina, to the river-god Aſopus.

Amazons from the banks of the Thermodon were said to have fought agatnsi the Greeks on the side of the Tro-jans.

GRANT, oh golden-ſpindled Graces, per-fuaſive ſplendour to the lay which the violet-crowned Muſes' inſpired prieſt prepares to ſing of Phlius and the fertile plain of Neme-aean Zeus: where white-armed Hera reared of old, firſt occaſion for Heracles of glorious exploit, a flock-flaughterer, deep-voiced lion. There crimfon-fliielded demigods, picked band of Argives, held the firft games over the tomb of young Archemorus, flain as he gathered flowers by felon fnake with yellow-flafhing eyes, an omen of impending overthrow. Oh refift-lefs power of fate! Did not Oecleus' fon urge them to march back to their warlike homes? Hope often gives ill counfel. She it was who then fent againft Thebes Talai'onid Adraftus, leagued with fteed-borne Polynices, after thofe famed contefts in the fields of Nemea. Illuftrious are the mortals who bind their auburn locks with the triennial wreath. Fortune now hath granted that boon to victorious Auto-medes, pre-eminent among the athletes of the pentathlum as is among the ftars, when the month is halved, the full-orbed moon: fo goodly a form he fhowed to encircling hofts of Hellas when he threw the rounded discus; or when the dark-leaved aflh's ftem hurled by his hand through the sky called forth applauding fhouts or when, in the clofing wreftle's lightning flafhes, with the fame tranfcendent ftrength he flung to earth his ftrong-limbed adverfaries ere he returning fought the dark-whirling waters of Afopus. That river's name hath travelled to all regions and as far as the fources of the Nile. Even the dwellers by the fair ftream of Thermodon, fkilled javelin-hurler daughters of fleet-fteeded Ares, rued, oh famous river, the prowefs of a child of thy flood beneath the lofty towers of Troy. To every region on broad highways travel myriad tales of thy race of ample-veftured daughters whom the gods with happy deftiny have feated on the thrones of unconquerable nations. Who hath not heard of Thebe of the hyadnthine locks and her well-built towers ? . . .

VI

The ode, of which the following passage is a fragment, celebrated the victory of Pytbeas, an Aegine-tan, in the boys' pancratium at Nemea. This victory is also celebrated in an extant ode of Pindar.

In the beginning of the ode Teirefias has a pro phetic vision of the victory of Heracles over the Nemean lion, and the infiitution of the Nemean games.

HE shall stay the tyrant's lofty insolence, and give justice to the world. How insupportable a hand the child of Perseus lays upon the neck of the devouring lion with exhaust-less resource, when his glittering death-dealing steel cannot pierce the unyielding hide, and the blade bends backward! Truly I predict that spot shall one day witness much-sweated con-tests of Hellenic champions for the wreaths of the pancratium . . .

[After mentioning the Aegnetan hero, Ajax, grandon of Aeacus, the poet then proceeds:

Who, stationed on his vessel's stern, stayed bold Hector of the brazen helm fiercely bent, though he was, on destroying the ships with horrid fire; what time the son of Peleus, nursing wrath, left the field and released the Dardan host from its terrors. Till then, panic-stricken, they ventured not to leave Dion's fair bulwarks, but crouched behind them, dreading the fierce shock of battle, so long as Achilles madly raged in the plain, shattering their ranks with brandished, host-slaughtering spear. But when the battle saw no more the violet-crowned

Nereid's dauntlefs fon : as on the darkling waters Boreas furioufly aflaults with whelming waves feafaring men whom he furprifes refting from their toils by night, but ceafes to ftorm when the light of morning breaks: a calm fmooths the billows: and, the South wind bellying the fails with its breath, the gladdened failors reach the defpaired of harbour : fo the Trojans, when they heard that the grim Achilles was ftaying in his tent becaufe of lovely yellow-haired Brifeis, lifted thankful hands to heaven, feeing war's ftorm-cloud fringed beneath with aufpidous light. Then, leaving with all hafte the walls of Laomedon, they rufhed into the plain, bringing vaft array of war, and ftruck terror into the Danai, urged on by javelin-hurler Ares and the lord of Lycia, Loxias Apollo. They reached the fhore and fought by the (hips' fair fterns, and blood of men flain by hands of He&or reddened the dark foil...

...They weened that they would deftroy the blue-prowed fhips and all their crews, and that on the morrow the found of joy and revelry would fill the god-built ftreets of Ilion. But fate ordained that, ere that hour arrived, the whirling waters of Scamander fhould be empurpled with their blood as they died by Aeacid hands, overthrowers of their towers ...

VII.

This fragment beging with the story of Io.

There are myride paths of deathlefs song for whofo has received gift from the Pieran Muses, and whofo hymns are clothed with fplendour by the violet-eyed, wreath-dispensing Graces. Weave now, oh commened Phantasy of a Cean bard, some novelty concerning lovely, heaven-favour Athens. Endowed by Calliope with her choicest gifts, it befeems thee of all others to soar a wondrous flight.

Once upon a time leaving Argos land of fleet fteeds, Inachus' rosy-singers child was fleeing far, by the will of mighy Zeus, blest potentate, transformed into a cow with golden horns : and Argus, whofe unworried eyes looked every way, was bidden by majeftic, golden-mantled Hera, uncouchingly, unsleepingly, to guard the heifer of the lovely horns. Not even Maia's son could elude his watchful gaze either by the bright-rayed day or the shades of holy night. But whether fate ordained that the swift messenger of Zeus should slay the monster-breeding Earth's fell offspring, Argus, or his never-resting watch outwearied him at last, or soothing strains of the Pierides closed his eyes in slumber, my surest way of shunning error is only to relate the end. After Io, bearing Epaphus in her womb, had reached the flowered banks of Nile, Zeus made her child ruler of linen-stoled priests, lord of peerless wealth, and founder of a mighty clan. From Epaphus sprung Agenor's scion, Cadmus, sire of Semele in seven-gated Thebes. She gave birth to the inspirer of the frenzied Bacchae, Dionysus [giver of the vine] and inventor of the wreath-crowned dance …

VIII

This ode celebrates a chariot victory of Hiero at Olympia, 468 B.C., won the year before his death.

CHOOSE fertile Sicily's queen, Demeter, and her violet-crowned daughter for the theme of thy fong, melodious Clio, and the fleet Olympic-racer fteeds of Hiero. For with tranfcendent victory and grace they flew along the broadly-whirling Alpheus, winning wreaths for Dinomenes' heaven-favoured fon. And Achaean ranks exclaimed: 'Thrice happy man who, by Zeus invefted wideft ruler of Hellenes, has the wifdom not to hide his high-piled wealth behind a dark obfcuring fhroud. The temples are aftir with feftive facrifices of oxen, the ftreets with hofpitality; and bright flafh the conizations from the gold of deepchased tripods, fet before the fhrine where the holieft grove of Phoebus by Caftalia's ftream is miniftered by Delphic priefts.'

Heaven, Heaven demands a tribute from every fortune-favoured mortal. For in bygone days horfe-taming Lydia's monarch, when by Zeus' fatal ordinance Sardis fell before the Perfian hoft, Croefus was prote&ed by the golden-fworded god, Apollo. When the grievous day arrived, the king was not one to await the added woe of a flave's all-tearful doom, but reared a pyre before the brazen walls of his palace-court, and mounted thereon with his confort dear and fair-haired, wildly weeping daughters. And, raifing his hands towards the o'er-canopying heaven, he cried reproachfully: ' Oh, overmaftering fupernal power, where is the gratitude of all the gods? Where is Latona's princely fon? . . . [Lydian blood ftains] the golden-fanded Pactolus. Lydian dames are ignominioufly torn from well-built homes. The hated foe is henceforth to be their dear lord. No! death is a fweeter lot.' So faying he bade kindle the gorgeous-carpeted wooden ftru&ure. His daughters fhrieked and flung their hands about their mother's neck: for horrid to mortals is the face of imminent death. But when the fierce fire's gleam began to penetrate the pile, Zeus brought overhead an abyfs of darkfome cloud, and quenched the yellow flamc. Incredible is nought that the divine will works. Thereupon the Delian god Apollo bore the old king to the Hyperboreans, and enthroned him in their midft with his taper-ankled daughters in requital of his piety, becaufe that of all mortals he had fent the richeft offerings to god-haunted Pytho . . .

King Apollo, the herdsman god, once told the son of Pheres: 'Mortal as thou art thou must nurse two expectations: that tomorrow's solar ray is the last which thou shalt see; and that thou shalt count another fifty years of happy life' Live righteously and joyously; this is highest wisdom. The wife will under-stand these words: The depths of ether have no stain; the water of the sea no corruption; gold is cheerer of the heart; and to man it is not given to cast off hoary eld and recover youthful days. But virtue's radiance dims not with the mortal frame's decay. It is nurtured by the muse. Hiero, thou hast shown the world prosperous fortune's fairest flowers. A bright career receives not his due meed from silence; and one of those who aim aright will be he who shall sing the honeyed strains of the Cean nightingale.

IX.

This fragment related to the demand addressed to the Trojans for the restoration of Helen. The Grecian embassy was introduced by Antenor, of whom we read in Vergil: 'Antenor potuit mediis elapses Achivis Illyricos penetr are sinus.' His son were worshipped as heroes at Cyreens. They give the ode its title, Antenoridae.

THEIR fire, prudent hero, bore to royal Priam and his sons all the massage of the Achaeans. Then heralds speeding through the wide-spread city fummoned the Trojan tribes to the people's meeting place. Every-where ran the tidings loudly-voiced, and hands uplifted to the immortal gods prayed that their troubles soon might an end. Say, mufe, whofe tongue first urged the plea of right. Pleisthenid Menelaus uttered winning words counselled by the fair-robed Graces.

'Oh warlike Trojans, it is not high-ruling and all-feeing Zeus that is the caufe to men of their calamities; for all mankind are free to hold faft to ftraight-walking Juftice, companion of chafte Order and wife Law. Happy they whofe children choofe to have this dweller in their ftreets! But the who flourilhes by treacherous falfehood and bold contempt of equal meafure, nought-reverencing Arrogance, firft lightly gives away another's wealth and havings, and after plunges into deep difafter. She it was that brought annihilation on the oveweening race of Earth-born giants .. '

IX

The following fragment fhows that the plot of the Trachiniae, a play which fome attribute to Sophocles, others to Iophon, his lefs-gifted fon, had been already outlined in the verfes of Bacchylides.

SUCH was the ftrain that Delphic choirs fang before thy far-famed fhrine, oh Pythian Apollo. Already Oechalia, faid the lay, had been left a flaming ruin by Amphitryo's dauntlefs fon, when he touched at the Euboean promontory, purpofing to offer from his fpoils nine deep-voiced bulls in facrifice to cloudy-throned Kenaian Zeus, two to the god who lifts the fea and fhakes the earth, and to Athena, ftern-eyed virgin, a fingle heifer, unyoked, lofty-horned. Then an overmaftering power infpired Deianira with a plan, that coft her many tears, to recover her confort's love, after fhe heard the cruel tidings that white-armed Iole was on her way, sent under escort to his palace as a lovely bride by Zeus' dreadless son. Ah, hapless wife! Ah, evil-starred! How direful was her deed! Malevolence of a mighty one wrought her ruin, and darkness shrouding future days, when on the rushing waters of Lycormas she took into her hands a fatal gift from Nessus....

www.bookjungle.com *email: sales@bookjungle.com fax: 630-214-0564 mail: Book Jungle PO Box 2226 Champaign, IL 61825*

The Codes Of Hammurabi And Moses
W. W. Davies

The discovery of the Hammurabi Code is one of the greatest achievements of archaeology, and is of paramount interest, not only to the student of the Bible, but also to all those interested in ancient history...

Religion **ISBN:** *1-59462-338-4* Pages:132 MSRP $12.95

QTY

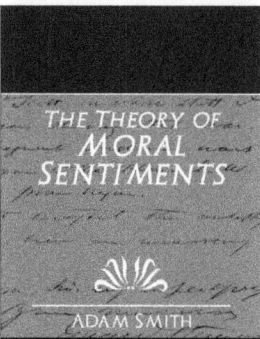

The Theory of Moral Sentiments
Adam Smith

This work from 1749. contains original theories of conscience amd moral judgment and it is the foundation for systemof morals.

Philosophy **ISBN:** *1-59462-777-0* Pages:536 MSRP $19.95

QTY

Jessica's First Prayer
Hesba Stretton

In a screened and secluded corner of one of the many railway-bridges which span the streets of London there could be seen a few years ago, from five o'clock every morning until half past eight, a tidily set-out coffee-stall, consisting of a trestle and board, upon which stood two large tin cans, with a small fire of charcoal burning under each so as to keep the coffee boiling during the early hours of the morning when the work-people were thronging into the city on their way to their daily toil...

Childrens **ISBN:** *1-59462-373-2* Pages:84 MSRP $9.95

QTY

My Life and Work
Henry Ford

Henry Ford revolutionized the world with his implementation of mass production for the Model T automobile. Gain valuable business insight into his life and work with his own auto-biography... "We have only started on our development of our country we have not as yet, with all our talk of wonderful progress, done more than scratch the surface. The progress has been wonderful enough but..."

Biographies/ **ISBN:** *1-59462-198-5* Pages:300 MSRP $21.95

QTY

www.bookjungle.com email: sales@bookjungle.com fax: 630-214-0564 mail: Book Jungle PO Box 2226 Champaign, IL 61825

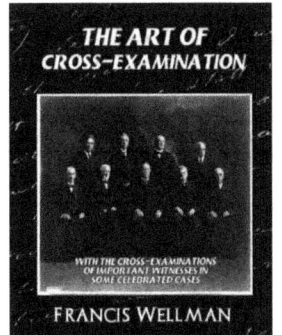

The Art of Cross-Examination
Francis Wellman

QTY

I presume it is the experience of every author, after his first book is published upon an important subject, to be almost overwhelmed with a wealth of ideas and illustrations which could readily have been included in his book, and which to his own mind, at least, seem to make a second edition inevitable. Such certainly was the case with me; and when the first edition had reached its sixth impression in five months, I rejoiced to learn that it seemed to my publishers that the book had met with a sufficiently favorable reception to justify a second and considerably enlarged edition. ..

Reference   ISBN: *1-59462-647-2*   Pages:412   MSRP *$19.95*

On the Duty of Civil Disobedience
Henry David Thoreau

QTY

Thoreau wrote his famous essay, On the Duty of Civil Disobedience, as a protest against an unjust but popular war and the immoral but popular institution of slave-owning. He did more than write—he declined to pay his taxes, and was hauled off to gaol in consequence. Who can say how much this refusal of his hastened the end of the war and of slavery ?

Law   ISBN: *1-59462-747-9*   Pages:48   MSRP *$7.45*

Dream Psychology Psychoanalysis for Beginners
Sigmund Freud

QTY

Sigmund Freud, born Sigismund Schlomo Freud (May 6, 1856 - September 23, 1939), was a Jewish-Austrian neurologist and psychiatrist who co-founded the psychoanalytic school of psychology. Freud is best known for his theories of the unconscious mind, especially involving the mechanism of repression; his redefinition of sexual desire as mobile and directed towards a wide variety of objects; and his therapeutic techniques, especially his understanding of transference in the therapeutic relationship and the presumed value of dreams as sources of insight into unconscious desires.

Psychology   ISBN: *1-59462-905-6*   Pages:196   MSRP *$15.45*

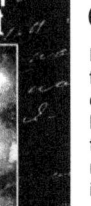

The Miracle of Right Thought
Orison Swett Marden

QTY

Believe with all of your heart that you will do what you were made to do. When the mind has once formed the habit of holding cheerful, happy, prosperous pictures, it will not be easy to form the opposite habit. It does not matter how improbable or how far away this realization may see, or how dark the prospects may be, if we visualize them as best we can, as vividly as possible, hold tenaciously to them and vigorously struggle to attain them, they will gradually become actualized, realized in the life. But a desire, a longing without endeavor, a yearning abandoned or held indifferently will vanish without realization.

Self Help   ISBN: *1-59462-644-8*   Pages:360   MSRP *$25.45*

www.bookjungle.com email: sales@bookjungle.com fax: 630-214-0564 mail: Book Jungle PO Box 2226 Champaign, IL 61825

QTY

	Title	ISBN	Price
☐	**The Rosicrucian Cosmo-Conception Mystic Christianity** *by Max Heindel* *The Rosicrucian Cosmo-conception is not dogmatic, neither does it appeal to any other authority than the reason of the student. It is: not controversial, but is: sent forth in the, hope that it may help to clear...* New Age/Religion Pages 646	ISBN: 1-59462-188-8	$38.95
☐	**Abandonment To Divine Providence** *by Jean-Pierre de Caussade* *"The Rev. Jean Pierre de Caussade was one of the most remarkable spiritual writers of the Society of Jesus in France in the 18th Century. His death took place at Toulouse in 1751. His works have gone through many editions and have been republished...* Inspirational/Religion Pages 400	ISBN: 1-59462-228-0	$25.95
☐	**Mental Chemistry** *by Charles Haanel* *Mental Chemistry allows the change of material conditions by combining and appropriately utilizing the power of the mind. Much like applied chemistry creates something new and unique out of careful combinations of chemicals the mastery of mental chemistry...* New Age Pages 354	ISBN: 1-59462-192-6	$23.95
☐	**The Letters of Robert Browning and Elizabeth Barret Barrett 1845-1846 vol II** *by Robert Browning and Elizabeth Barrett* Biographies Pages 596	ISBN: 1-59462-193-4	$35.95
☐	**Gleanings In Genesis (volume I)** *by Arthur W. Pink* *Appropriately has Genesis been termed "the seed plot of the Bible" for in it we have, in germ form, almost all of the great doctrines which are afterwards fully developed in the books of Scripture which follow...* Religion/Inspirational Pages 420	ISBN: 1-59462-130-6	$27.45
☐	**The Master Key** *by L. W. de Laurence* *In no branch of human knowledge has there been a more lively increase of the spirit of research during the past few years than in the study of Psychology, Concentration and Mental Discipline. The requests for authentic lessons in Thought Control, Mental Discipline and...* New Age/Business Pages 422	ISBN: 1-59462-001-6	$30.95
☐	**The Lesser Key Of Solomon Goetia** *by L. W. de Laurence* *This translation of the first book of the "Lemegton" is now for the first time made accessible to students of Talismanic Magic was done, after careful collation and edition, from numerous Ancient Manuscripts in Hebrew, Latin, and French...* New Age/Occult Pages 92	ISBN: 1-59462-092-X	$9.95
☐	**Rubaiyat Of Omar Khayyam** *by Edward Fitzgerald* *Edward Fitzgerald, whom the world has already learned, in spite of his own striving, to look upon as one of the rarest poets of the century, was born at Bredfield, in Suffolk, on the 31st of March, 1809. He was the third son of John Purcell...* Music Pages 172	ISBN: 1-59462-332-5	$13.95
☐	**Ancient Law** *by Henry Maine* *The chief object of the following pages is to indicate some of the earliest ideas of mankind, as they are reflected in Ancient Law, and to point out the relation of those ideas to modern thought.* Religion/History Pages 452	ISBN: 1-59462-128-4	$29.95
☐	**Far-Away Stories** *by William J. Locke* *"Good wine needs no bush, but a collection of mixed vintages does. And this book is just such a collection. Some of the stories I do not want to remain buried for ever in the museum files of dead magazine-numbers an author's not unpardonable vanity..."* Fiction Pages 272	ISBN: 1-59462-129-2	$19.45
☐	**Life of David Crockett** *by David Crockett* *"Colonel David Crockett was one of the most remarkable men of the times in which he lived. Born in humble life, but gifted with a strong will, an indomitable courage, and unremitting perseverance...* Biographies/New Age Pages 424	ISBN: 1-59462-250-7	$27.45
☐	**Lip-Reading** *by Edward Nitchie* *Edward B. Nitchie, founder of the New York School for the Hard of Hearing, now the Nitchie School of Lip-Reading, Inc, wrote "LIP-READING Principles and Practice". The development and perfecting of this meritorious work on lip-reading was an undertaking...* How-to Pages 400	ISBN: 1-59462-206-X	$25.95
☐	**A Handbook of Suggestive Therapeutics, Applied Hypnotism, Psychic Science** *by Henry Munro* Health/New Age/Health/Self-help Pages 376	ISBN: 1-59462-214-0	$24.95
☐	**A Doll's House: and Two Other Plays** *by Henrik Ibsen* *Henrik Ibsen created this classic when in revolutionary 1848 Rome. Introducing some striking concepts in playwriting for the realist genre, this play has been studied the world over.* Fiction/Classics/Plays 308	ISBN: 1-59462-112-8	$19.95
☐	**The Light of Asia** *by sir Edwin Arnold* *In this poetic masterpiece, Edwin Arnold describes the life and teachings of Buddha. The man who was to become known as Buddha to the world was born as Prince Gautama of India but he rejected the worldly riches and abandoned the reigns of power when...* Religion/History/Biographies Pages 170	ISBN: 1-59462-204-3	$13.95
☐	**The Complete Works of Guy de Maupassant** *by Guy de Maupassant* *"For days and days, nights and nights, I had dreamed of that first kiss which was to consecrate our engagement, and I knew not on what spot I should put my lips..."* Fiction/Classics Pages 240	ISBN: 1-59462-157-8	$16.95
☐	**The Art of Cross-Examination** *by Francis L. Wellman* *Written by a renowned trial lawyer, Wellman imparts his experience and uses case studies to explain how to use psychology to extract desired information through questioning.* How-to/Science/Reference Pages 408	ISBN: 1-59462-309-0	$26.95
☐	**Answered or Unanswered?** *by Louisa Vaughan* *Miracles of Faith in China* Religion Pages 112	ISBN: 1-59462-248-5	$10.95
☐	**The Edinburgh Lectures on Mental Science (1909)** *by Thomas* *This book contains the substance of a course of lectures recently given by the writer in the Queen Street Hall, Edinburgh. Its purpose is to indicate the Natural Principles governing the relation between Mental Action and Material Conditions...* New Age/Psychology Pages 148	ISBN: 1-59462-008-3	$11.95
☐	**Ayesha** *by H. Rider Haggard* *Verily and indeed it is the unexpected that happens! Probably if there was one person upon the earth from whom the Editor of this, and of a certain previous history, did not expect to hear again...* Classics Pages 380	ISBN: 1-59462-301-5	$24.95
☐	**Ayala's Angel** *by Anthony Trollope* *The two girls were both pretty, but Lucy who was twenty-one who supposed to be simple and comparatively unattractive, whereas Ayala was credited, as her Bombwhat romantic name might show, with poetic charm and a taste for romance. Ayala when her father died was nineteen...* Fiction Pages 484	ISBN: 1-59462-352-X	$29.95
☐	**The American Commonwealth** *by James Bryce* *An interpretation of American democratic political theory. It examines political mechanics and society from the perspective of Scotsman James Bryce* Politics Pages 572	ISBN: 1-59462-286-8	$34.45
☐	**Stories of the Pilgrims** *by Margaret P. Pumphrey* *This book explores pilgrims religious oppression in England as well as their escape to Holland and eventual crossing to America on the Mayflower, and their early days in New England...* History Pages 268	ISBN: 1-59462-116-0	$17.95

www.bookjungle.com email: sales@bookjungle.com fax: 630-214-0564 mail: Book Jungle PO Box 2226 Champaign, IL 61825

QTY

The Fasting Cure by *Sinclair Upton* ISBN: *1-59462-222-1* **$13.95**
In the Cosmopolitan Magazine for May, 1910, and in the Contemporary Review (London) for April, 1910, I published an article dealing with my experiences in fasting. I have written a great many magazine articles, but never one which attracted so much attention... New Age/Self Help/Health Pages 164

Hebrew Astrology by *Sepharial* ISBN: *1-59462-308-2* **$13.45**
In these days of advanced thinking it is a matter of common observation that we have left many of the old landmarks behind and that we are now pressing forward to greater heights and to a wider horizon than that which represented the mind-content of our progenitors... Astrology Pages 144

Thought Vibration or The Law of Attraction in the Thought World ISBN: *1-59462-127-6* **$12.95**
by *William Walker Atkinson* Psychology/Religion Pages 144

Optimism by *Helen Keller* ISBN: *1-59462-108-X* **$15.95**
Helen Keller was blind, deaf, and mute since 19 months old, yet famously learned how to overcome these handicaps, communicate with the world, and spread her lectures promoting optimism. An inspiring read for everyone... Biographies/Inspirational Pages 84

Sara Crewe by *Frances Burnett* ISBN: *1-59462-360-0* **$9.45**
In the first place, Miss Minchin lived in London. Her home was a large, dull, tall one, in a large, dull square, where all the houses were alike, and all the sparrows were alike, and where all the door-knockers made the same heavy sound... Childrens/Classic Pages 88

The Autobiography of Benjamin Franklin by *Benjamin Franklin* ISBN: *1-59462-135-7* **$24.95**
The Autobiography of Benjamin Franklin has probably been more extensively read than any other American historical work, and no other book of its kind has had such ups and downs of fortune. Franklin lived for many years in England, where he was agent... Biographies/History Pages 332

Name	
Email	
Telephone	
Address	
City, State ZIP	

☐ Credit Card   ☐ Check / Money Order

Credit Card Number	
Expiration Date	
Signature	

Please Mail to: Book Jungle
PO Box 2226
Champaign, IL 61825
or Fax to: 630-214-0564

ORDERING INFORMATION

web: *www.bookjungle.com*
email: *sales@bookjungle.com*
fax: *630-214-0564*
mail: *Book Jungle PO Box 2226 Champaign, IL 61825*
or PayPal *to sales@bookjungle.com*

Please contact us for bulk discounts

DIRECT-ORDER TERMS

20% Discount if You Order Two or More Books
Free Domestic Shipping!
Accepted: Master Card, Visa, Discover, American Express

www.ingramcontent.com/pod-product-compliance
Lightning Source LLC
Chambersburg PA
CBHW081330040426
42453CB00013B/2372